Greek Mythology

The complete guide to Greek Mythology, Ancient Greece, Greek Gods, Zeus, Hercules, Titans, and more!

Copyright 2015

Table Of Contents

Introduction 1
Chapter 1: Greek Mythology 3
Chapter 2: Greek Gods 5
Chapter 3: The Characters of Greek Mythology 9
Chapter 4: Hercules 30
Chapter 5: Perseus 36
Chapter 6: The Titans 41
Chapter 7: The Trojan War 50
Chapter 8: Pygmalion and Galatea 54
Chapter 9: Hyacinth 56
Chapter 10: Procne and Philomena 59
Chapter 11: Prometheus and Pandora 63
Conclusion 66

Introduction

I want to thank you and congratulate you for purchasing the book, "Greek Mythology – The 2nd Edition".

This book contains helpful information about Greek Mythology, the history behind it, and some of the great Greek mythology stories.

You will discover tales of Hercules, Zeus, Prometheus, and more. These ancient stories have been passed down for thousands of years, and have been the inspiration for many movies and stories that we have today.

As you will soon realize, sayings such as 'opening Pandora's box', and 'Achilles heel' are also the result of some Greek mythological stories. You will discover the stories behind these sayings, along with several other important moments in Ancient Greek mythology.

You will learn the history of the ancient Greeks and Romans, and be left with a greater understanding and appreciation of Ancient Greek culture, lifestyle, and beliefs.

As you read on, you will learn of the most notable stories in Greek Mythology, including the 12 labors of Hercules, the famous Trojan War, and how fire was introduced to man.

This is the second edition of this popular book on Greek Mythology. In the update, an additional 6 chapters have been added, and the book has been more than doubled in length. This updated version really is the complete guide to Greek Mythology!

Thanks again for downloading this book, I hope you enjoy it!

Chapter 1: Greek Mythology

The mythical stories of ancient Greece have an enduring power that has allowed them to survive from long ago in around 900 B.C. and be re-told countless times until today. It may come as a surprise to most people that many of our beloved contemporary literature, films and shows are simply re-tellings and adaptations of these stories. The names, settings, situations and plots may change, but many of our stories can trace back their roots to Greek Myths.

We continue to discover these tales of heroic adventure and divine folly from Greek literature and art. Literary sources that many are familiar with would be the epic poems of Homer, the *Iliad* and the *Odyssey*. Other sources are Hesiod's *Theogony*, which gives the most complete account of Greek creation myths, the origins and genealogies of gods, Titans and Giants, and other folktales. Hesiod also wrote *Works and Days* that includes the tales of Prometheus and Pandora, which you will encounter later in this book. Aside from poetry, Greek drama was largely inspired by myths. Theater plays were often offered to the gods and performed during sacred feasts. One of the world's greatest tragedies, Oedipus, is also found in this book.

Archaeological sources have also uncovered these myths that would otherwise have been lost to time. They also help in elaborating and answering some questions that have been posed based on the literary sources. Many Greek artefacts show representations of deities and events from mythical tales told in the oral-poetic tradition. Western art throughout the ages has also been largely inspired by scenes from these tales. The two most major archaeological finds are the discoveries of Heinrich Schliemann in the 19th century and of Sir Arthur Evans in the 20th century. The evidence found in the unearthing of the Mycenaean civilization and the Minoan civilization, respectively, provide us details about deities, heroes, rituals and practices of the ancient Greeks.

The history of the world as told in mythology can be classified into three periods. The first is the Age of the Gods from the beginning of time and the creation of the world and humankind. The second is the Age of Gods and Mortals when men interacted with deities, also resulting in demigods. The third is the Age of Heroes where the focus is more on the acts of men with some divine intervention.

The study of Greek Mythology is significant because it sheds light on the political and social milieu of ancient Greek society and of this particular period in our history. It also helps us understand the nature of myth-making and recurring themes in our tales that date back centuries ago. They illustrate how people look at the world around them, its origins and creations, and explain occurrences they encounter in their life like death, war and disease, and even more beautiful situations like birth, marriage and love.

Chapter 2: Greek Gods

Hellenistic religion is polytheistic where the ancient Greeks worshipped many gods. It is also animistic with their beliefs of deities being rooted in the nature and everyday life that they encounter.

The Greek immortals can be classified under several categories. There are the mighty Olympians, the lesser Titans, the Giants and other deities. The twelve Olympian deities are considered the most sacred and powerful of them all.

At the head of them is Zeus who is considered to be the supreme ruler of Mount Olympus. He is the god of the sky. Thunder and lightning is attributed to him. He is also the god of justice. His sacred animals are the bull and the eagle. Zeus is often depicted as an old but strong man of regal poise wielding a lightning bolt. In Roman religion, he is known by the name Jupiter.

His brother is Poseidon, god of the sea and earthquakes. He is often depicted like his brother Zeus; mature, sinewy and with a glorious beard. However, he holds a trident. His sacred animals are the horse and the dolphin. In Roman religion, he is known as Neptune.

Hades is the ruler of the underworld and the god of death. He is brother to Zeus and Poseidon. He is often depicted with a cornucopia and the three-headed dog Cerberus who guards the entrance to the underworld. The Romans referred to him as Pluto.

The three brothers rule over the three domains of the universe: the sky, the sea, and the underworld.

Hera is Zeus' consort and queen of the Olympians. She is the goddess of women, childbirth and marriage. She is often depicted as a regal woman. She is known in many Greek myths to cause trouble due to her husband's many infidelities. The peacock and the cuckoo are sacred to her. She is known by the name Juno in Roman religion.

Aphrodite is known as the goddess of love and beauty. Myth has it that she was born from sea foam from which her name is derived from. She is depicted as a very beautiful woman and myths suggest that she had many lovers, though she was forced by Zeus to marry Hephaestus, who was known to be ugly and deformed. This was done to prevent the disruption of peace among the gods, who might fight over her. Aphrodite's equivalent in Roman religion is Venus. Animals sacred to her are sparrows and doves.

Considered to be Zeus' favorite daughter who was born from his forehead, Athena is the goddess of wisdom and warfare. She is depicted in a war helmet and wielding a spear and shield. She has a long history of being a patron of heroes. Athena is also linked to the city of Athens. Her sacred animal is the owl. The Romans called her Minerva.

Apollo is the god of the arts. He is depicted in art as a handsome young man playing the lyre amongst the Muses. His sacred animals are the swan, deer and fox. He is also known as Apollo to the Romans.

His twin sister is Artemis who is the goddess of hunting and the wild. She is depicted as a young woman with a bow and arrow. Her sacred animals are mostly wild animals. She is known by the name Diana in Roman religion.

Ares is the god of war and violence. He is depicted as a warrior in armor or a nude young man with a helmet and shield. Unlike Athena who symbolizes strategy involved in war, he symbolizes the chaos that ensues. He also had an affair with the wife of his brother Hephaestus, Aphrodite. His sacred animals are the snake, boar and vulture. In Roman religion, he is known as Mars.

The goddess of agriculture is Demeter who is depicted as an older woman holding wheat. Pigs and snakes are sacred animals to her. In Roman religion, she is known by the name Ceres.

Dionysus is the god of wine, feasts and other pleasures. He is always depicted with a cup of wine or grapes and a crown of leaves and flowers. Serpents and tigers are sacred animals to him. The Greeks also called him Bacchus, a name which is also used by the Romans. It refers to the frenzy he brings. He has cult followers who believe in ecstasy and freedom from any restraints.

Hephaestus is the god of metalwork, crafting and fire. He is the crippled husband of Aphrodite. He is usually depicted with a hammer and anvil, like a smith. The donkey is sacred to him. In Rome, he is known as Vulcan who is feared for his volcanic power.

The virgin goddess Hestia is worshipped for the home. She is often depicted as a modest, veiled woman. Hestia gave up her position as an Olympian and Dionysus replaced her. She is known as Vesta in Rome.

The Titans were the gods before the Olympians, but were eventually overthrown in the War of the Titans or the Titanomachy. There were twelve original Titans, namely Iapetus, Crius, Cronus, Coeus, Hyperion, Oceanus, Themis, Rhea, Phoebe, Theia, Tethys and Mnemosyne. The next generation was comprised of Hyperion's children Eos, Selene and Helios; Iapetus' children Prometheus, Epimetheus, Atlas and Menoetius; Coeus' children Asteria, Leto and Lelantos; Crius' children Pallas, Perses and Astraeus; Oceanus' child Metis.

Notable of these is Helios who is the Titan of the sun and is known to ride a chariot that carries the sun across the sky. Atlas was the Titan forced by Zeus to carry the sky on his shoulders. Prometheus is the god who granted man the secret of fire.

Chapter 3: The Characters of Greek Mythology

The Twelve Olympians

Zeus

Zeus was the ruler of all gods of Mount Olympus. He is the god of sky and thunder, and is the youngest son of Titans Cronus and Rhea. His parents were siblings and the children of Uranus and Gaia. Zeus married Hera and had three children – Ares, Hebe and Hephaestus. His other children from numerous consorts were Aecus, Athena, Apollo, Artemis, Aphrodite, Dardanus, Dionysus, Hermes, Heracles, Helen of Troy, Perseus, and Minos along with the Graces and the Muses. The king of all gods was known also as the god of law and order and was often depicted with a thunderbolt in his hand.

Zeus was prophesized to become the ruler of Olympus in place of Cronus even before he was born. Cronus was told that he would be replaced by his son. Not wanting to let go of his crown, he ate all of his children. When Rhea gave birth to Zeus, she hid the infant and gave Cronus a rock wrapped in swaddling clothes instead. Like with his other children Cronus swallowed the rock thinking it was his child. Rhea hid Zeus in a cave in Crete where he was raised by Gaia. One version of the story says that Zeus was raised by Amalthea in the Psychro Cave. Another claims Adamanthea hung Zeus from a tree in a way that Cronus could not see him. Other personalities who supposedly raised the god were the nymph Cynosura, Melissa, and a family of shepherds.

Zeus eventually confronted his father and forced him to disgorge his brothers and sisters. One popular version says that Zeus cut open Cronus' stomach. Another said an emetic was used. Cronus first spewed out the stone, and then his children (in reverse order as they were born). Afterwards, Zeus freed Cronus' brothers along with the Gigantes, Hecatonkheires and the Cyclopes. Zeus received his famous thunder and lightning from the Cyclopes.

Hera

Hera, the Queen of the Gods, is the goddess of marriage, birth and women. She is consort to Zeus, her brother. She bore six children – Ares, Hebe, Eileithyia and Hephaestus with Zeus, while she also had Enyo and Eris. In other stories, her children were not conceived with Zeus or any man but instead by slapping the ground. Others say that eating a lettuce led her to give birth to her children. It is believed that the deity regains her virginity every time she bathes in the spring of Canathus.

When Hera had Hephaestus, she despised the infant for its ugliness and threw him out of Olympus. Later on, Hephaestus would take his revenge by trapping her on a throne he made. Once Hera sat on the throne, she could not get off. Hera was only able to get off the chair after Dionysus took a drunken Hephaestus back to Olympus after he refused to do so of his free will. He asked for Aphrodite to be his consort in exchange for releasing Hera.

Hera not only despised her own child, she was also jealous of Zeus' other consorts and his children with them. The goddess tried and failed to stop the birth of Apollo and Artemis. Even the hero Heracles who was named after her didn't escape the goddess' wrath. She tried to prevent his birth by tying his mother Alcmene's legs together. Her plan didn't work because her servant Galanthis made her believe that Alcmene already gave birth. To punish Galanthis, Hera turned her into a weasel. The angered goddess put a couple of serpents in Heracles' cradle to kill him but the infant strangled them. Hera also made life difficult for Io and Dionysus. She sent a giant with a hundred eyes to guard Io while she made Dionysus' foster parents go mad.

Poseidon

The God of the Sea is known by many names. While popularly called Neptune in Roman mythology, Poseidon is also referred to as Hippios or Lord of Horses and Enosichthon or Earth-shaker. He is one of the more popular gods in Greek mythology and is often depicted with a trident in his hand. Poseidon was the son of Cronus and Rhea, and had Hestia, Demeter, Hera, Hades, and Zeus as his siblings. After the siblings overthrew Cronus, they divided the universe among themselves. Zeus became ruler of the heavens, Hades ruled the Underworld while Poseidon became king of the sea.

Poseidon rode on a chariot pulled by magnificent horses while sailors often sacrificed horses in his name in exchange for a safe voyage at sea. These are the reasons for why he is known as the Lord of Horses. However, sometimes those sacrifices were not enough to appease the god. He is known for his volatile temper, which usually causes storms and earthquakes. He once caused the Attic Plain flood because the people admired Athena more than him, even after he created the Acropolis Spring for the people.

Poseidon sired a number of children. He had Triton, a merman, and Benthesikyme with Amphitrite, Pegasus and Chrysaor with Medusa, Dictys with Agamede, and twins Pelias and Neleus with Tyro. He was a staunch admirer of his sister Demeter who transformed into a mare to escape the sea god's advances. But that did not deter Poseidon as he turned himself into a stallion and forced himself on the mare. Their union bore them the talking horse Arion (Areion). They also had Despoina. Poseidon also forced himself on Caenus and Amymone whom he rescued from a satyr, and Aethra who gave birth to Theseus. Atlas is one of five sets of twins Poseidon sired with the mortal Cleito. His other children were Nauplius (with Amymone), Agenor, Belus, Neleus and the cyclops Polyphemus. He is also believed to have sired King Amycus, King Busiris, Eumolpus, Orion, Pelias, and the Giant Sinis, among many others.

Demeter

Demeter was a favorite among the mortals. She is the goddess of fruitfulness and planned society. The fertility goddess showed the mortals how to sow and plough... Demeter, which means "mother goddess", proved her motherly love when a love-struck Hades kidnapped Demeter's daughter Persephone, with Zeus, whom the King of the Underworld wanted as his wife. Demeter searched for nine days and nights during which the earth became barren. She transformed into an old woman named Doso and rested in the town of Eleusis. She was sitting by a well when the daughters of King Celeus found her and offered the old woman a place to stay and rest. The royal family was kind to the goddess and in return, she planned to make Queen Metanira's youngest son immortal. Demeter fed

Demophon (or Triptolemus) ambrosia and started burning his mortality in the hearth. A maid saw them one night and told the queen who cried out loud for her to stop (Another version says the maid herself was the one who shouted). The goddess revealed herself and told the queen that her son, while no longer can be immortal, will be a great hero.

Zeus finally intervened after the earth suffered from famine due to Demeter's grievance. He ordered Hermes to proceed to the Underworld and convince Hades to return Persephone. The god's daughter was returned but not before eating a pomegranate which Hades had given her. That act bound Persephone to stay with Hades a third of each year. Since then, Demeter would grieve during the time Persephone was with Hades and the earth would become barren during the same period.

Athena

Another one of the more popular deities, Athena was known as the goddess of wisdom, courage and strategic warfare. She also presided over the arts, crafts, law and justice, and skills. The Titan Metis was Zeus' first wife whom he swallowed out of fear of producing a son that was stronger than him. They had a daughter, Athena, who was born from Zeus' head. Zeus suffered from headaches while he was hammering a helmet he intended to give to Athena. Hephaestus split the god king's skull open to remedy the pain and from it sprang a full-grown Athena, adorned in her mother's robe and helmet.

The virgin goddess is loved by mortals and she has helped them in many ways. For one, the people in a Greek city chose her over Poseidon when she made the olive tree for them. The city was renamed Athens as a tribute to the goddess. Athena also aided a number of heroes during their exploits. She provided help to Perseus in slaying Medusa. Athena helped Argus build the ship (which she protected during its travels) used by Jason. She also enabled Bellerophon to tide Pegasus by providing him with a magic bridle. Athena was also involved in the Trojan War which was the result of a contest of beauty between three goddesses. She sided with the Greeks and was behind the famous wooden horse.

Apollo

Apollo and his twin sister Artemis were born from the union of Zeus and Leto. He was the god of truth, music and prophecy. He was also called Phoebus (god of light), Smintheus (rat) and Parnopius (grasshopper). Apollo also presided over archery, colonization, dance, intellectual inquiry, poetry, medicine, and plague.

Apollo and Artemis were born in Delos, a floating island then surrounded by swans. The island was later attached to the seabed by Zeus using four sturdy columns and became Apollo's sanctuary. A mere four days after he was born, Apollo slayed Python, the dragon which lived in Delphi (Pytho) and guarded the Castalian Spring. The dragon was sent by Hera to kill Leto but Apollo slayed it using Hephaestus' bow and arrows. Delphi later became another of Apollo's oracles. Unfortunately, Python was Gaia's son so Apollo was sent to become a cowherd of King Admentus for eight or nine years as punishment. Hera wasn't done yet. She then sent the giant Tityos to assault Leto. Apollo and Artemis joined hands in defending their mother. Zeus would then banish the giant to Tartarus.

Apollo was also known for his beauty and had many consorts (both men and women) and children. He fell in love with the handsome Hyacanthus who was tragically killed by a disc that the gods threw. Apollo's children include Aristaeus with Cyrene, Troilus with Hecuba (King Priam's wife), Ion with Creusa, and Asclepius with Coronis, among many others. Not all gave in to Apollo's charm. Cassandra, the daughter of Troy's King Priam, rejected the god and was punished. She had prophetic powers previously given to her by Apollo as a sign of his affection, but he made her be able to see only tragedies. Daphne, the nypmh daughter of the river god Ladon (others say Peneus), also refused the god's advances and transformed into a laurel tree to escape him. Others, like Coronis, were disloyal to the god. Coronis had an affair with Ischys while she was pregnant with Apollo's son. The crow (which used to have white feathers) tasked to guard Coronis was turned to black.

Artemis

Apollo's twin was the goddess of the wilderness, hunting, and fertility. Artemis was born a day before her twin brother (in most accounts) and was Leto's midwife when she gave birth to Apollo. Another telling of the story says Artemis helped Leto cross the straits of Delos so she could have Apollo there.

A virgin goddess like Athena, Artemis was one of the most respected of all gods. She was the patron of small children and women in childbirth. She was a healer like her brother, but also brought various diseases to the mortals. It was said that while a child, Artemis asked her father Zeus for six wishes. The first was to always remain a virgin. This is why she was also the patron of chastity. She punished any man who wished to end her purity. She once turned Actaeon into a stag simply because he chanced upon her and her nymphs bathing in their nakedness. There is one story about the attempted rape of Artemis. The goddess escaped unscathed after she killed the man who tried to assault her – Orion. Some say she killed him and his dog with her bow and arrow. Others say a scorpion which Artemis conjured killed them. Orion and his dog became a constellation of stars. Zeus once tricked one of Artemis' nymphs by disguising himself as the goddess herself. This allowed the god king to bed Callisto and produce a child -- Arcas. Angered, Artemis turned Callisto into a bear and killed her. She became the constellation we now know as The Great Bear.

Artemis was not only protective of her nymphs; she was also possessive of her stags and her sanctuaries. Agamemnon would find out the hard way after the hero killed one in Artemis' sanctuary. She punished Agamemnon by preventing his ships to travel to Troy. He was then forced to sacrifice his daughter, Iphigenia. Another version says he sacrificed a deer instead and made his daughter into a priestess that served the goddess.

Artemis had her share of adventures as a youngster. She became a great hunter after getting her bow and arrows in Lipara, an isle that Hepaestus and the Cyclops called home. She also asked the God of the Forest, Pan, for seven bitches and six dogs. Her chariot is drawn by six deers with golden horns which she captured herself.

Ares

Ares was the god of war. He was known for instigating violence, which didn't sit well with many of the deities. In fact, he was particularly despised by Zeus because of his hateful ways. Ares had two constant companions (his sons in most versions) during battles – Phobos and Deimos, the gods of fear and terror, respectively. Enyo (goddess of discord) was his lover who also accompanied him during wars, often seen riding in his famed chariot. His other companions during wars were Kydoimos, Polemos, the Makhai, and the Hysminai.

Ares had Aphrodite as one of his lovers. With her, he sired Eros, Anteros, Himeros, Pothos, Phobos, Deimos, Harmonia, and Adrestia. Aphrodite was the wife of Hephaestus, who got his revenge on the two erring lovers. With Aglauros, Ares sired Alcippe who was raped by Halirrhothius, Poseidon's son. This event led to the creation of the court of justice on Areopagus, also known as the Hill of Ares. Cycnus, Ares' son with Pyrene or Pelopia, took after his father. He slayed many and built a temple made of the skulls of his victims. Some of his other children were Ascalaphus and Ialmenus with Astyoche, Mygdon with the Muse Calliope, and Diomedes and Crestone with Cyrene.

Ares supposedly created the first rooster. He tasked Alectryon to warn him and Aphrodite once he saw Helios (who always dropped by to announce the sun's arrival) approaching. The young man fell sleep and allowed Helios to discover the lovers and report what he'd seen to Hephaestus. As punishment, Ares turned him into a rooster tasked to announce the sun's arrival each morning. The God of War was also involved in the creation of the lunar year. The giants Otus and Ephialtes once caught Ares and placed him inside an urn. The god suffered in the urn for thirteen months until he was rescued by Hermes with the help of the giants' mother Eriboea. Ares sided with the Trojans during the Trojan War in which he was defeated by Athena and the Greeks.

Aphrodite

The goddess Aphrodite was born from the sea foam created after Uranus' genitals were thrown into the sea by Cronus. She was the goddess of love and lust whose main 'function' was to mate. She had in her possession a special girdle that enabled anyone who wore it to be desirable. Aphrodite used the girdle on a number of mortals resulting in many a god falling in love with these mortals.

Zeus had her marry the ugly Hephaestus to prevent any war between the gods over her beauty. But that did not deter the goddess from having numerous affairs with gods and mortals.

Aphrodite was caught in a love triangle with her husband Hephaestus and lover Ares. The former devised a plan to catch the lovers and ridicule them. She and Ares, both naked, were caught in a net made by her husband and were exposed to their fellow gods. Poseidon and Hermes were smitten by the naked goddess. The God of the Sea proposed that Ares pay for all the gifts Zeus received in marriage from Hephaestus after the cuckolded god demanded their return. Poseidon, as guarantor, would pay what Ares failed to pay in exchange for Aphrodite becoming the Sea God's wife, which eventually did happen. Hermes, meanwhile, asked Zeus for help after the goddess rejected him. Zeus had Aphrodite's sandal stolen and, in exchange for its return, had to lay with Hermes who sired Hermaphroditus with her.

Among Aphrodite's other consorts were Adonis, Anchises, and Dionysus. Her children, aside from those she had with Ares and Hermes, were Thalia, Euphrosyne and Aglaea with Dionysus, Beroe, Golgos and possibly Priapus with Adonis, and Aeneas and Lyrus with Anchises. Others believed to be her children were Meligounis, Peitho, Eryx, Tyche, Astynoos, Rhode, and Tyche.

Aphrodite supposedly caused the death of Hippolytus. Aphrodite admired the hero, but he preferred Artemis. Because of this, the goddess of love made his stepmother fall for him. Phaedra took her own life after her stepson rejected her. This eventually led to his death.

Hephaestus

The god of craftsmanship is known for his 'ungodly' looks and for being wronged by his wife Aphrodite who had many affairs, the most notable of which was with Ares. He found out about Aphrodite's wrongdoings when Helius saw her and Ares in the latter's palace in Thrace (or in the hall of Hephaestus in some accounts). To get his revenge, Hephaestus created a bronze net, which he secretly attached to his bed. He left the next morning and returned to find his wife and Ares, both naked, caught in the net. He had the other gods come and see the two humiliated lovers.

Aside from Aphrodite, he had Aglaea, Aetna and Caberio as consorts. Among his children were Thalia, Eucleia, Eupheme, Philophrosyne, Cabeiri, Euthenia, Palici, Periphetes, Ardalus, Olenus, Philottus, Pylius, Spinter, and Palaemonius. He supposedly had a child with Gaia by accident named Erichthonius. He was supposed to have union with Athena but the goddess refused. Athena disappeared and Hephaestus' ejaculate fell on the earth, making Gaia pregnant in the process.

Hephaestus was an expert in creating weapons, which he provided to all the Olympian gods.

Hermes

The union of Zeus and the nymph Maia produced Hermes, the herald of Mount Olympus. His grandparents were Atlas and Pleione. Story goes that while everyone else was asleep, Zeus visited Maia in a cave on Mount Cyllene and got her pregnant.

Come morning, Hermes was already born. While his mother was sleeping, Hermes ran away and found himself in Thessaly where he stole some cattle from Apollo's herd. The young god hid the cattle in Greece before returning to his mother but not before slaying a tortoise. He also killed one of Apollo's cows and made his first lyre from its intestines and the tortoise's shell. A commotion ensued with Apollo blaming Hermes for his missing cattle and Maia defending her supposedly sleeping son. During the argument, which now involved the king god Zeus who witnessed Hermes' wrongdoings, the young god started playing his lyre. Everyone was enchanted with the music, especially Apollo. He gave Hermes the cattle he took in exchange for the lyre, which eventually became one of Apollo's symbols. Hermes not only invented the lyre but also the flute and syrinx. He got his heralds staff from Apollo who exchanged it with Hermes' flute. The cunning god is also credited for inventing boxing and running races.

Hermes is the god of trade, land travel, border crossings or boundaries, shepherds, merchants, athletes, thieves, sports, literature, oratory, poetry, and weights and measures. He is not only the messenger of gods but also a guide of the Underworld.

Hermes sired Abderus, the half-man half-goat Pan with Dryope, and the two-sexed Hermaphroditus with Aphrodite. Hermes provided Perseus with his winged sandals in the hero's quest to slay Medusa. The god also freed Zeus' lover Io from the giant Argus. The swift-moving god also helped Odysseus while he was a captive of Calypso and during the hero's plight against Circe.

Hestia

Hestia is the first child born to Cronus and Rhea. While she was the first to be born, Hestia was also considered the youngest as she was last to be freed from Cronus' stomach. Hestia was the goddess of domestic life. She guarded the sacred hearth fire in the hall of Olympus. She kept the fire alive by feeding it with the animal sacrifices offered to them. The gentle virgin goddess also presided over architecture, the family, and the state.

Hestia is believed to be part of the Twelve Olympians but some accounts place Dionysius among the list instead. This may be attributed to the goddess' passiveness and kindness. It is said that she gave up her seat to Dionysus to avoid any confrontations among the Olympians. Another story describes Hestia's inability to leave the hearth fire, which may have led to Dionysius taking her seat among the gods.

Other Deities

Hades

The God of the Underworld is often confused as being one of the Twelve Olympians. The Lord of the Dead is the son of Cronus and Rhea. Along with his brothers Zeus and Poseidon, Hades divided the world among them. Zeus ruled the heavens or upper world while Poseidon claimed the seas. Hades, meanwhile, ruled the nether world. With him in the land of the dead were Thanatos, Hypnos, and Charon. Cerberus was tasked with guarding the gates of the Underworld.

Persephone

This goddess ruled the Underworld with her husband Hades. Persephone, daughter of Zeus and Demeter, was abducted by

Hades. Her absence caused the earth to be infertile as her mother Demeter grieved for her. Zeus, through Hermes, ordered Hades to release her but the goddess ate a pomegranate that bound her to stay in the nether world for a third of each year.

Heracles

One of the most popular Greek characters, Heracles (Hercules) has been the subject of numerous stories and adaptations. He was the son of Zeus and Alcmene and was known as the Gatekeeper of Olympus. He was the god of strength and divine protector of mankind. He was also the patron of heroes.

Heracles had a twin brother named Iphicles who was sired by Alcmene's husband Amphitryon who slept with her the same night Zeus, disguised as her husband, did. The Greek hero, who was christened Alcides, is known for his many exploits. As an infant, he strangled two serpents sent by Hera to kill him. Athena later took him to Hera who nursed the infant not knowing he was Heracles. The baby's suckling was so painful that Hera let him go abruptly causing her milk to scatter, thus creating the Milky Way. Hera's milk gave Heracles his super strength. Athena gave the baby back to Alcmene who raised him with her husband.

Heracles would go on to marry Megara. Hera, still angered with Heracles, caused him to go mad during which he killed his own children. He was healed of the lunacy and upon realizing what he did, asked help from the Oracle of Delphi. Guided by Hera, the oracle told Heracles to serve his rival King Eurystheus for ten years. The king gave him the task of finishing ten labors to cleanse him of his sin and to make him immortal. The cheating king later made it twelve. His twelve labors included the slaying of the Nemean Lion, the Lernaean

Hydra, and the Stymphalian Birds. He also had to capture the Golden Hind of Artemis, the Erymanthian Boar, the Cretan Bull, and Cerberus. Heracles also had to gather or steal the Mares of Diomedes, the girdle of Hippolyta, the cattle of Geryon, and the apples of Hesperides. He also had to clean the Augean stables in one day.

Popular Greek Heroes

Achilles

One of the main figures during the Trojan War, Achilles was the son of King Peleus and the nymph Thetis. As an infant, Achilles was dipped into the River Styx by Thetis to make him invincible. However, his heel, where Thetis held him, remained vulnerable. He was, fatally wounded when Paris, son of the Trojan king, shot an arrow to his heel.

Aeneas

Aeneas fought for Troy during the Trojan War and avoided being killed thanks to the gods particularly Aphrodite, Apollo and Poseidon. After the war, he fled and reached Italy where he founded the city of Rome.

Ajax the Great

The son of King Telamon and Peiboea, Ajax was a great warrior trained by the centaur Chiron. During the Trojan War, Ajax did not get any help from any of the gods but remained unscathed. He engaged Hector in a duel that ended in a draw due to the superior yet equal skills of both rivals. As a gesture of respect, they exchanged gifts. Ajax gave Hector his purple sash while he received Hector's sword. When Patroclus, wearing Achilles' armor was killed, Ajax and Odysseus work together to retrieve the magical armor. They later competed for the armor which was eventually awarded to Odysseus. A humiliated Ajax wanted to get revenge but was tricked by Athena into killing a flock of sheep. He realized what he had done and proceeded to take his own life out of shame.

Daedalus

Daedalus was a famous craftsman responsible for the Labyrinth on Crete and the dancing ground for Ariadne. But perhaps he is more known for creating the wings he and his son Icarus used to escape their tower prison. They were locked up to stop them from sharing details about the labyrinth. They were able to escape but his son flew too high and the wax he used to secure the feathers melted. His son plummeted to the sea and drowned. Athena later gave him real wings so he could fly like a god.

Hector

Another hero on the Trojan side, Hector was respected for his courage and nobleness. He was tasked to fight Achilles but fled in fear of the great Greek warrior. Hector ran around the city thrice before overpowering his fear and fighting Achilles. He kept on fighting even if he knew the Gods favored his rival.

Jason

Jason led 50 Argonauts in search of the Golden Fleece. King Pelias stole the kingdom from Jason but swore to return it if he succeeded in bringing him the Golden Fleece. The group faced many perils, including an encounter with Sirens, but eventually found the fleece. During his adventure, Jason met and fell in love with the sorceress Medea.

Odysseus

Odysseus, King of Ithaca, fought for the Greeks during the Trojan War. It took him ten years to travel back to his home after the war. The journey was filled with perils. He faced the Sirens, Polyphemus the Cyclops, and Scylla and Charybdis. Even upon reaching his home he had a minor adventure in proving his identity to his wife Penelope.

Orpheus

Orpheus, son of Apollo and Calliope, was known for traveling to the Underworld to retrieve his beloved wife Eurydice who died. Orpheus was such a genius in playing the lyre that his music greatly affected Hades. The King of the Underworld allowed the hero to take back his wife provided he walk in front of her without looking back. Before they could leave the land of the dead, Orpheus succumbed to the temptation and looked back at Eurydice. Because of this, his wife disappeared.

Theseus

Theseus was the son of King Aegeus of Athens though some say his father was Poseidon. The popular hero was among the fourteen people sent through the labyrinth occupied by the Minotaur. With the help of a magic ball of thread that was given to him by Ariadne, Theseus was able to slay the monster and escape the maze.

Monsters of Greek Mythology

Arachne

Arachne was a creature with half a body of a woman and half that of a spider. She was the mother of all spiders. She used to be a mortal woman but was turned into a monster by Athena after she boasted and lost to the goddess Athena in a weaving contest.

Caucasian Eagle

The giant eagle was tasked by Zeus to feed on the ever-regenerating liver of Prometheus. He is the son of Echidna.

Centaur

This creature had the head and upper body of a human and the lower body and legs of a horse.

Cerberus

The giant three-headed dog guarded of the gates of the Underworld.

Charon

He was ferryman at the river Styx.

Charybdis

This sea monster creates whirlpools when it inhales endangering any ship within the vicinity.

Chimera

The chimera is a three-headed (lion, snake, and goat) creature that breaths fire. It has lion claws in front, goat legs behind and the tail of a snake.

Empousai

Empousai are vampire demons that seduce then ensnare men before eating them. They had fiery hair, bronze legs and donkey's feet.

Erinyes

The Furies are the three goddesses of vengeance.

Gorgon

Gorgons are three monster sisters with snakes on their head and the ability to turn anything to stone. The most famous, Medusa, used to be a gorgeous woman with stunning hair. Her hair was turned into snakes by Athena after Medusa lain with (or was raped by) Poseidon inside the goddess' temple. Another version tells that Medusa was given the snakes by Athena to protect herself from men. Stheno and Euryale are the other two Gorgons.

Graeae

The Gray sisters were three old women with one tooth and one eye among them.

Harpies

This creature has the upper body, arms and head of a woman and the wings, tails and talons of a bird.

Lernaean Hydra

This serpent with many heads guarded the Underworld entrance beneath Lake Lerna. It was killed by Heracles.

Merpeople

They were people whose lower halves were fish tails.

Minotaur

The minotaur is one of the more popular creatures in Greek mythology. It has the head of a bull and body of a man.

Orthrus

Orthrus was a two-headed dog and the brother of Cerberus. He was killed by Heracles.

Panes

These nature-spirits had the head and torso of humans, and the legs and tails of goats. They also had goat horns on their heads.

Satyrs and Satyresses

These creatures accompanied Pan and Dionysus. They had the upper body of humans, and the horns and hindquarters of goats.

Scylla

Scylla was once a beautiful maiden and lover of Poseidon who was turned by Circe into a creature with many heads and tentacles. She feasted on sailors caught between herself and Charybdis.

Sirens

The deadly bird-like women lure sailors to their deaths with their songs.

Skolopendra

This sea monster as huge as a Greek trireme was the child of Phorcys and Keto.

Chapter 4: Hercules

Hercules is a great Hellenic hero and the ultimate symbol of manhood, strength and bravery. Known as a demigod, he is the illegitimate son of Zeus and the mortal Alcmene who was wife to a soldier named Amphitryon. He was born as a twin to Iphicles, who is Amphitryon's true biological son. Hera, knowing of Zeus' infidelity, is thought to be the cause behind the lifelong torment experienced by Hercules. The traditional spelling of his name is "Heracles" which was derived from "Hera" as his parent's act of respect and contrition to his namesake. However, Hera remained appeased.

As an infant, he was found in his cot by his nurse playing with snakes like they were children's toys. Curious about this incident, Amphitryon sought Tiresias, a seer who saw a future for the boy where he fought monsters.

The parable "The Choice of Hercules" tells a tale of Hercules in his youth. While he was tending cattle on a mountain, two nymphs appeared before him with two choices. The nymph Pleasure offered him a pleasant, simple life led by an easy path. On the other hand, the nymph Virtue offered him a harsh life that will eventually lead to glory.

Hercules went to Thebes and married the daughter of King Creon named Megara. Hera, not pleased, decided to bestow upon him a fit of rage. He went mad and killed all of his six children and Megara. After his madness was cured, he was shocked by what he has done and decided to flee Thebes. He found the great Oracle of Delphi who told him what he must do. The oracle, under the influence of Hera, instructed him to serve the new King Eurytheus, his cousin and old rival, and do everything he was told to do. Only then will he be cleansed of his sin and become immortal. Eurytheus ordered him to perform ten labors, and added two more to what literature now refers to as "The Twelve Labors of Hercules" or the dodekathlon.

The first labor was to slay the Nemean lion that abducted women and took them to its lair to encourage warriors to save them. As a warrior enters the cave, he would find an injured woman who will suddenly turn into a lion and kill him. His bones will be given to Hades. In the town of Cleonae, Hercules met a shepherd whose son was taken by the lion. He then went off to rescue the boy and sacrifice the lion to Zeus. When he found the lion, he fired arrows at it. Unfortunately, the lion's fur could not be penetrated by weapons. Afterwards, the lion retreated back to its cave. Hercules blocked one of the two entrances to the lion's cave and went through the other. Trapping the lion inside, Hercules clubbed the lion to death. He attempted to skin the animal, but its hide could not be penetrated by his knife. He tried to sharpen the knife on a stone and even used the stone to no avail. Athena saw Hercules' trouble and helped him by telling him to use one of the lion's claws. Hercules' armor is made out of the Nemean lion's hide. He carried back the remains of the lion to King Eurystheus who set him off to his next task.

The second labor was to slay the Hydra, a monster raised by Hera herself for the sole purpose of defeating Hercules. It lived in a swamp at Lake Lerna that spewed poisonous gas. Hercules drew the Hydra out of its dwelling cave. He took his sword and cut off its head. Unfortunately, two more heads grew in its place. He cut off its heads and found the two more would grow out in each place. He cut them again and again to the same result. Seeing that he was not winning against the Hydra, he sought the help of his nephew Iolaus who figured that he should scorch with a firebrand each neck stump after cutting. Eventually, only one head was left, its sole immortal one. He took this head and buried it under a rock. He proceeded to dip his arrows into the Hydra's poisonous blood and completed his task. King Eurytheus did not accept that Hercules fulfilled this task because he had the help of Iolaus.

The third labor was specially designed by King Eurystheus and Hera to defeat Hercules. Since it had been made clear that Hercules was good at slaying beasts, they set him out to a different kind of task. He was told to catch the Ceryneian Hind which could run very fast. Hercules spotted the hind and chased it on foot for one whole year. He passed through Thrace, Greece, Istria and the Hyperborean Land. He finally caught it by trapping it under a net as it slept. The hind is an animal sacred to Artemis. She was angered by Hercules' action and confronted him. This was all part of King Eurytheus' plan all along and he expected the goddess to punish him. He apologized and promised to return the hind after he has used it to fulfill his task. Artemis allowed him to do so. He took the hind to King Eurytheus and was informed that it was to become part of the royal menagerie. Hercules told the king to take it himself from him if he wanted it. When Hercules released the hind, it escaped the king and quickly ran back to Artemis, keeping Hercules' promise to her.

The fourth labor was similar and Hercules had to again take back a beast to the king. This time, it was the Erymantian Boar. Hercules sought the help of the great centaur Chiron in capturing the boar. Chiron advised him to lead the boar into thick snow. Hercules successfully caught the boar this way and took it back to King Eurytheus who was very afraid of the beast and told Hercules to take it away. He followed and threw the beast into the sea. It is told that the beast swam all the way to Italy.

The fifth labor was for Hercules to clean the Augean stables. It was meant to simply humiliate Hercules because the animals in the stables were immortal and managed to produce a lot of dung throughout their long lives. There were around a thousand cattle. Hercules fulfilled the task by redirecting the Rivers Alpheus and Peneus to wash away the dung and dirt that had accumulated in the stables. Augeas, who promised Hercules a tenth of his cattle if he were to finish the task in a day, became furious and refused to keep his end of the deal because he found out that the task was an order of King Eurytheus. Hercules killed him and gave his kingdom to Phyleus, his exiled son. King Eurytheus did not consider the task fulfilled because he was paid for the task.

The sixth labor was to beat the Stymphalian birds which were ferocious birds that devoured men, had beaks and feathers made of metal that could be shot like an arrow, had poisonous droppings, and were sacred to the god of war, Ares. They were considered pests as they were fast breeders and destroyed fruit-bearing trees and crops and attacked people. Athena gifted Hercules with a rattle that would frighten the birds. He used it and was able to shoot them in the air with his poison arrows. The rest who survived fled and never came back.

The seventh labor was to capture the Cretan Bull which was terrorizing the island of Crete. Hercules found the bull, rode it and choked it right up to the point before death. He sent it back to King Eurytheus who decided to sacrifice it to Hera.

Hera refused the sacrifice which signified Hercules' triumph. It was released and came upon Marathon where it would later be caught and sacrificed to the gods by Theseus.

The eighth labor was to steal the Mares of Diomedes. The mares were dangerous creatures that breathed fire and ate human flesh. With the help of youths, Hercules took the mares and they were chased by Diomedes and his men. Hercules fought Diomedes and fed his corpse to his own horses. He found that eating made the mares calmer, so he was able to bind their mouths closed. He brought them back to King Eurytheus. It is believed that the horses were the ancestors of horses used in the Trojan War. This will be discussed in the next chapter.

The ninth labor was to steal the Girdle of Queen Hippolyta, which was a gift from Ares to the queen of the Amazons. It was desired by Admete, the daughter of King Eurytheus. Hercules set off for the land of Themiscyra where the Amazons lived. Hippolyta had heard of Hercules' exploits and was very impressed with him. She would easily have given him the girdle had it not been for Hera who disguised herself as an Amazon and planted vicious rumors about Hercules, including plans of abducting their queen. When the Amazons confronted Hercules in a battle, he suspected treachery and killed the queen, stole her girdle and took it back to King Eurytheus.

The tenth labor was to catch the Cattle of Geryon on the island of Erytheia. On the way, he passed the Libyan Desert. In his frustration with the heat, he shot an arrow towards the Sun, at Helios. The god admired his bravery and granted him the golden cup he uses to travel from the west to the east every day. Hercules used the cup to reach Erytheia in the east. When he got there, he had to fight a two-headed watchdog, Orthrus, and a herdsman, Eurytion. Geryon also confronted him but was killed with Hercules' poison arrows. Hercules took the cattle back to King Eurytheus. On the way, Hera ordered a gadfly to bite the cattle and cause madness among the herd. They scattered and Hercules took after them for a year. Hera also raised the river they were crossing, so Hercules had to pile rocks into the river where the cattle could cross. They eventually reached King Eurytheus and the cattle was sacrificed to Hera.

The eleventh labor was to steal the Apples of the Hesperides. The Hesperides were nymphs who tended a garden in a far corner of the world where golden apples grew. They gave immortality to anyone who ate the apples. In the Garden of the Hesperides, Hercules was able to trick the god Atlas into getting the apples for him while he held the sky up for the god.

The twelfth labor was to capture Cerberus, the three-headed dog that guarded the entrance to the underworld. Hercules discovered the entrance with the aid of Athena. He found the god Hades and asked if he could bring Cerberus back to the surface. Hades agreed on the condition that he capture the dog without the use of any weapons. Being very strong, he was able to fight and catch the beast with his bare hands. He brought Cerberus back to King Eurytheus who was very frightened of the beast and ordered him to immediately take it back to the underworld. Finishing the last task, he was then relieved from his labors.

Chapter 5: Perseus

Perhaps one of the more popular mortal Greek characters was Perseus. He was the son of Zeus and Danae, the daughter of King Acrisius of Argos. Perseus came from a line of royalty. Acrisius was the son of Abas, the twelfth king of Argos, and Aglaea. Abas, meanwhile, was the son Lynceus who was the son of Danaus. Acrisius was not as fortunate as his ancestors as he failed to conceive a son and future king. In desperation, he went to the Oracle of Delphi to seek answers. What he got was something he never would have thought of.

The legend of Perseus started when King Acrisius was told of a prophecy by the Oracle that he would perish at the hands of his own grandson. According to Apollo, Acrisius' daughter Danae was to give birth to a son who would eventually take the king's life. Horrified, King Acrisius had his daughter locked up in a tower. He threw the key away to make sure no one could get in or out of the tower. There were no doors on the bronze tower. There was, however, a small window. Another version indicates that Danae was kept in a bronze chamber that was "open to the sky" and located in the middle of the king's courtyard.

The Olympian god Zeus saw Danae's predicament. He changed himself into a shower of gold and entered the tower through the window. He showed himself to Danae who described the figure to be a man with a thunderbolt in his hand. Zeus offered to turn her dark prison into a sunny and more livable place. In exchange, she was to be his wife. Danae agreed and she instantly found herself in a beautiful field comparable to those in Elysium. As prophesized, Danae bore a son with Zeus.

Acrisius eventually discovered the birth of the infant Perseus when he chanced upon the tower one time and saw light coming out from the window and had his men demolish a portion of the wall of the tower so he could see what was happening inside. He was fearful of Zeus so instead of killing the infant, he placed Danae and Perseus in a wooden chest and let them drift out to sea.

Mother and son reached Seriphos unscathed. Dictys, the brother of King Polydectes, discovered them in the chest and set them free. He raised the boy who grew up to be a resilient young man. When Polydectes proposed and was rejected by his mother, he tried to get rid of Perseus so he could force Danae to marry him. The king held a feast and asked the guests to bring horses as gifts to Hippodamia whom he claimed he was going to propose to. The king knew very well Perseus did not have any horse or treasure. The king sent Perseus on a mission to slay the Gorgon Medusa and bring him her head as a gift. Hermes and Athena who despised the Gorgon appeared before Perseus and offered help. They also revealed to him that they were siblings. They instructed him to seek the Hesperides who have in their possession a special pouch or knapsack that will hold Medusa's head. Athena herself provided the hero with a mirrored shield. Other gods chipped in. Hermes let him borrow his pair of winged sandals while Zeus provided him with an adamantine sword. A different telling of the story states that Hermes lent the hero the sickle that Cronus castrated Uranus with. Perseus also had Hades' helm of darkness, which he could use for hiding. To find the nymphs, Perseus had to seek Atlas who provided him with the whereabouts of the Graeae who, in turn, had knowledge of the Hesperides' location. Perseus travelled to the western end of the earth to find Atlas who showed him where the Gray Sisters were. Perseus had to seize the sisters' lone eyeball to force them to take him to the nymphs. Perseus received the pouch (some say they also gave him the helm or cap of darkness).

Once in Medusa's cave, Perseus used the polished shield to look around. In the shield's reflection, he saw Medusa sleeping. He took this opportunity to chop off her head using Zeus' sword and place it in the pouch. Pegasus and his brother Chrysaor, Medusa's sons, came out of the Gorgon's severed neck. Perseus fled the cave but was chased by Medusa's immortal sisters Stheno and Euryale. He escaped using the helm of darkness. A different account of the story states that Perseus only met Atlas after he fled from the Gorgons. It is believed that Atlas refused to accommodate the lost hero so Perseus turned him into stone using Medusa's head. Another story tells that Perseus took pity on Atlas and turned him to stone so the Titan would feel no more pain from carrying the heavens.

Perseus stopped by Aethiopia after spying a statue-like figure chained to a rock. Aethiopia was ruled by King Cepheus and his wife Cassiopeia. The queen boasted that their daughter Andromeda was as beautiful as the Nereids, which didn't sit well with Poseidon. The angered god sent Cetus, a sea serpent, to wreak havoc in Aethiopia. To appease the god, a naked Andromeda was tied to a rock as sacrifice to Cetus. Perseus flew using his winged sandals (or rode the winged Pegasus according to some) to slay Cetus and set the princess free. He then asked for Andromeda's hand. Their marriage infuriated Phineus, son of Belus and brother of King Cepheus, because

Andromeda was promised to him. Phineus, who did nothing during Andromeda's ordeal, started to quarrel with Perseus and even threw his spear at the hero. Perseus fought bravely but was surrounded by Phineus' men. He then used Medusa's head to turn them into stone.

Perseus went to Tyrins in Argos with Andromeda. There they had a son and named him Perses. On his way back to Seriphos, he flew over Libya. Drops of blood from Medusa's head fell on the sand and turned into venomous serpents. Others say that the couple went directly to Larisa where Perseus either participated in the games (particularly the discus throw) or introduced the quoit to everyone. The quoit is a game he invented that involved the throwing of petal rings. It was said that Acrisius, who exiled himself in fear of Perseus going to Argos or was exiled by Proteus, was killed by either the discus or metal ring Perseus threw. Some also say that Perseus turned Proteus to stone after he found out that the king exiled Acrisius. He also turned Acrisius to stone after the latter doubted his slaying of medusa. He was supposed to be named king but refused and made Megapenthes, Acrisuis' son, king.

Perseus finally returned to Seriphus only to discover that the king never married and his mother was made handmaiden by Polydectes. The hero left Andromeda under Dictys' care while he fled to the palace and turned Polydectes to stone. Dictys was made king of Seriphus while Andromeda and Perseus settled and started a new family. They had nine children -- sons Heleus, Perses, Alcaeus, Sthenelus, Mestor, Cynurus, and Electryon, and daughters Autochthe and Gorgophone. Perseus was great grandfather of Heracles. It is said that Perseus was the founder of Mycenae through Electryon.

Perseus death has many versions as well. One story claims that he died in the hands of Dionysus. Another says the god did not slay Perseus but did engage in war with him when the hero prevented Dionysus from entering Argos. During the fight, Perseus killed Ariadne. The more accepted version of his death was that Perseus died of old age. Perseus and Andromeda were later turned into stars.

Chapter 6: The Titans

The Twelve Uranides

Cronus

Cronus or Kronos was known as the king of the Titans. The first generation Titan became ruler of the universe after overthrowing his father Uranus with the help of his brothers Coeus, Crius, Hyperion and Iapetus. He was the one who castrated Uranus using a stone sickle given to him by his mother Gaia. The youngest of the twelve Titans, Cronus married his sister Rhea and had six children – Demeter, Hestia, Hera, Hades, Poseidon, and Zeus. Cronus was fearful of his children as it was said that one of his children will eventually overthrow him. Because of this, he swallowed his children right after they were born. Zeus was last to be born, and Rhea, not wanting her child to be devoured by his father, devised a plan to prevent this with Gaia's help. Rhea wrapped the Omphalos stone in a swaddle and handed it to Cronus who swallowed it. Zeus was saved from this fate and eventually dislodged Cronus from his throne. Zeus was able to free his brothers and sisters by slicing his father's stomach open.

After Cronus and the other Titans lost in the Titanomachy, most of them were banished to Tartarus by Zeus. Another tale signifies that Cronus was imprisoned in Nyx. He was said to be released by Zeus and appointed King of Elysium.

Oceanus

Oceanus was the eldest child of Uranus and Gaia. He was the personification of the ocean, the vast river that circles the Earth. He sired the Oceanids and all the rivers on Earth including Thetis, Metis, Amphitrite, Dione, Pleione, Nede, Nephele, Amphiro, Inachus, Amnisos, and the Potami by his sister and consort Tethys.

Oceanus was known for not taking part in the Titanomachy. He, along with Proetheus and Themis preferred to stay away from the war between the Titans and Olympians. It is also believed that he refused to join his brothers in overthrowing and castrating their father Cronus.

Iapetus

Iapetus, known as the Piercer as his name implies, is thought of as the Titan god of craftsmanship because of his connection to the spear. He is, however, more known as the Titan god of mortality. Iapetus had Clymene (or Asia) as a wife with whom he fathered Atlas, Menoetius, Prometheus, and Epimetheus. The Titan was involved in the dethronement of their father Cronus and was since banished to Tartarus by Zeus after the war between the Titans and Olympians.

Iapetus is considered by some as the ancestor of mankind. The mortals were direct descendants of his four sons and acquired the four Titans worst qualities – the daringness of Atlas, Menoetius' arrogance and propensity to be violent, the slyness and scheming ability of Prometheus, and Epimetheus' ineptness, guilelessness, and stupidity.

Hyperion

Hyperion's name stands for "the High One" or "he who goes before the sun". Hyperion was one of the brothers who ended Uranus' reign. The Titan is the father of Helios, Selene and Eos with his sister Theia. Hyperion was often confused with his son Helios. Hyperion is the Titan god of watchfulness, wisdom and light, while his son is the personification of the Sun.

Coeus

Coeus was the son of Uranus and Gaia who was responsible, along with three of his brothers, for holding their father while Cronus castrated him. He was one of the four pillars, along with Crius, Hyperion, and Iapetus, that kept heaven and earth separate. Coeus was sent to the Underworld after the Titans' defeat at the hands of the Olympians. He was able to break free from his chains but was unable to escape due to Cerberus. Coeus was also known as Koios and was the Titan god of intellect and inquisitive minds. He had his sister Pheobe as his wife by whom he sired Asteria and Leto.

Crius

Crius, the Titan god of constellations, was one of the four brothers who conspired against their father Uranus. Also called Kreios and Krios, he was considered the Titan god of measuring the duration of the year. He was the south pillar that parted the heaven and earth. Crius consorted with Eurybia and had three children -- Astraios, Pallas and Perses. He was one of the Titans banished to Tartarus after the ten-year long Titanomachy.

Rhea

Rhea is the daughter of Uranus and wife of Cronus. She had six children – the gods Poseidon, Hades, Demeter, Hestia, Hera, and Zeus. As the Mother of the Gods, Rhea was enraged with her husband's decision to swallow their children. Fed up with the practice, Rhea wrapped a large stone in swaddling clothes and gave it to Cronus who instantly devoured it. This allowed her youngest, Zeus, to survive and later rescue his brothers and sisters.

Tethys

The Titaness Tethys, whose name means "the nurse" in Greek, is the physical incarnation of the fertile ocean. She is the wife of Oceanus with whom she had more than 3000 children. Among her children were the Potamio or the rivers, the Oceanides or the springs and streams, and the Nephelai or the clouds. Tethys is the Tiran goddess of the different fresh water sources.

Theia

Theia also goes by Thea and Thia. The Titaness' name means "goddess" or "divine". She is the consort of her brother Hyperion with whom she had Helios, Selene, and Eos.

Phoebe

Phoebe was the Titan goddess of prophecy. Her marriage to her brother Coeus bore her daughters Leto and Asteria who gave the Titaness her grandchildren -- Apollo, Artemis, and Hectate. Phoebe used to own the oracle of Delphi which was passed on to Apollo.

Themis

The Titanness is the personification of the divine right order and natural law. Themis was the one who first organized the "communal affairs of humans". She was also capable of foreseeing and was once one of the Oracles of Delphi. She supposedly gave the oracle to Phoebe who, in turn, handed it down to Apollo whose birth at Delos the Titan goddess witnessed.

Themis was married to Zeus and bore the Horae and the Astraea. Some believe that Zeus sired the Moirai with Themis.

Mnemosyne

Mnemosyne was the Titan goddess of memory and the one who invented words. She gave birth to the nine Muses from her union with Zeus that lasted for nine consecutive nights. There was a river in Hades named after her where the souls of the dead were asked to drink from.

The Four Iapetionides

Atlas

Atlas is one of the more popular Titans. He is the son of Iapetus and Clymene. He is depicted as a man carrying a sphere on his shoulders. According to Greek mythology, Atlas was punished by Zeus for his role in the Titanomachy. He led the Titans in battle against the gods of Olympus. When his side lost, Zeus made him carry the sky to avoid the primordial embrace between the Heavens and the Earth.

The Titan god of astrology and navigation married Phoebe and sired Calypso, Dione, Hesperides, Hyas, Maera, the Hyades, and the Pleiades, among others. Perseus turned Atlas to stone using Medusa's severed head either in retaliation for not being hospitable to the mortal or because Perseus pitied the Titan and wanted to release him from his painful burden. Perseus descendant Heracles later asked the Titan to get the golden apples from Hera's garden. Atlas tried to fool Heracles into permanently replacing him in carrying the sky but Heracles didn't fall for it.

Prometheus

Prometheus was the one who created mankind. He is also popular for his slyness and once fooled the other gods, Zeus included, into devouring bare bones of cattle instead of their meat, which he gave eternally to mankind. This started the practice of sacrificing inedible parts of animals wrapped in fat while the mortals kept the meat for themselves. Furious, Zeus withdrew the human's ability to use fire. Prometheus then stole the sacred fire in Mount Olympus and gave it to the mortals. Of course, the god was even more enraged by this. He sent Pandora, the first of womankind who was made by Hephaestus from clay and given life by the four winds, to earth as punishment for mankind.

Prometheus sided with the Olympians during the Titanomachy but had a falling out with Zeus after his misdeeds and after the fact that he failed to inform the god of a prophecy that one of Zeus' sons would dethrone the Olympian ruler. Because of this, the king god banished the Titan to Caucasus where he was chained to a rock for eternity. Zeus, not contented, ordered an eagle to feast on Prometheus' liver every day since his liver regenerated each night. Prometheus would be freed from his fate by Heracles.

Epimetheus

The name of this Titan means "afterthought" or "hindsight". The foolish Epimetheus is the opposite of his brother Prometheus who was deemed clever. The brothers were tasked to provide mankind and other animals with positive attributes. Prometheus delivered by entrusting them with the ability to use fire and civilizing arts. Epimetheus, not planning his moves, entrusted every animal with a positive trait but left none for humans thus the trait of lacking foresight. If that wasn't enough, the Titan god took Pandora, the all-gifted, as his wife. When Pandora was sent to the world be Zeus, she had with her a jar or box that contained all kinds of evil.

Menoetius

His name means "doomed might" which may explain why he was killed by Zeus by a thunderbolt during the Titanomachy. Menoetius was the Titan god of hasty actions and intense anger.

Other Titans

Asteria

Asteria was the goddess of the night, nocturnal prophecies and shooting stars. The young Titan was the mother of Coeus and Phoebe. Asteria married Perses and they had Hecate. Leto is her brother. Zeus was smitten by her after the Titans fell. She became the island of Delos after she jumped into the sea to escape Zeus. The alternative to this story is that Asteria turned into a quail before falling and becoming the quail island, Ortygia.

Astraeus

Also known as Astraios, the young Titan was the god of stars, dusk, winds and astrology. He is the son of Crius and Eurybia. Astraeus married Eos and sired the four directional winds known as Anemoi and the five wandering stars or Astra Planeta.

Clymene

Borne to Oceanus and Tethys, Clymene was the goddess of fame, infamy, and renown. She was the wife of Iapetus and gave birth to Atlas, Epimetheus, Prometheus, and Menoetius. She also had Phaeton and the Heliades with Helios.

Dione

Dione was an Oceanid or water nymph who brought Aphrodite into the world. Her name is derived from the female version of Zeus or "dios".

Eos

She was the personification of dawn. She was the consort of Astraeus who fathered the four winds – Boreas, Eurus, Zephyrus, and Notus -- by her. She was the one who opened heaven's gates to allow the Sun to proceed. Eos became a nymphomaniac when Aphrodite exacted revenge on her for sleeping with Ares. She also had Orion, Cephalus and Tithonus as consorts.

Metis

Metis is considered as Zeus' first wife who gave birth to Athena. She was the physical incarnation of wisdom.

Ophion

He once ruled Olympus along with Eurynome. He was later banished to Tartarus.

Pallas

Pallas was born to Crius and Eurybia and had Styx as his consort. He sired Zelus, Mike, Cratos and Bia. In one story, Athena killed Pallas after he tried to force himself on her. The goddess then created the Aegis from his skin.

Selene

Selene was the goddess of the moon. She had many consorts including Endymion, Pan and Zeus. Selene seduced and had a union with the shepherd Endymion with whom she had fifty daughters.

Styx

Stxy was the goddess of the river of death that goes by the same name as hers. The river was located in the nether world.

Chapter 7: The Trojan War

The Trojan War was waged by the Greeks against the city of Troy, when Paris of Troy took the Spartan Queen Helen from her husband King Menelaus. The best source for this tale can be found in the epic poem Iliad by Homer.

It all began when the goddesses Hera, Athena and Aphrodite were quarreling due to the actions of the goddess Eris, who liked to sow conflict. Eris became outraged when she was not invited to the wedding of Peleus and Thetis. At the banquet, she threw onto the table a golden apple with the marking "For the fairest." This apple is known in literature as "The Apple of Discord" which sparked the beginning of the Trojan War. The three goddesses all wanted the apple for themselves. To settle the dispute, Zeus sent the women to Paris who was asked to judge who among them were indeed the fairest and should rightfully receive the apple. They each gave him a promise in exchange for the apple. Hera told him that she will grant him power; Athena will give him wealth; Aphrodite promised him the most beautiful woman in the world. Paris judged that Aphrodite was the fairest of them. He proceeded to set out to capture Helen, the wife of King Menelaus of Sparta. Paris took Helen back to Troy and married her.

Menelaus was outraged by what happened and called onto his warriors to honor their oaths and help him take back what is his. Achilles was one of the warriors who joined the cause. A Greek fleet then set off to sail for Troy. The phrase "the face that launched a thousand ships" is attributed to the beautiful Helen of Troy.

The city was difficult to find and they managed to first land in Mysia. The Greeks thought that it was the Teuthranians who had taken Helen and proceeded to attack the city. The king of the Teuthranians, Telephus, was severely wounded in the war by Achilles. The Greeks won the war but they suffered many casualties, and not knowing where else to head to, they went back home.

King Telephus went to Greece to get his wound cured after an oracle told him that the only person who could cure him was the one who wounded him in the first place. Achilles helped him and in return, Telephus told them how they can reach Troy.

Menelaus and Odysseus went to King Priam of Troy and demanded that Helen along with other goods stolen by Paris be returned to them. The king refused them and Menelaus decided that war was the only way.

In the first nine years of the war, the Greeks attacked the neighboring kingdoms of Troy from which it receives its supplies. Throughout the war, the Greeks won many battles but they were still unable to bring down the mighty, fortified walls of Troy.

Notable episodes from the decade-long war include the death of the Trojan hero Hector who was killed by Achilles. In his grief from the death of Patroclus, his trusted companion, at the hands of Hector, Achilles tied Hector's corpse to his chariot and dragged his body around the walls of the city.

The great Achilles was eventually killed when Paris shot an arrow through his heel. The term Achilles heel is a reference to this moment and pertains to a person's weakness. Achilles is the son of the nymph Thetis who dipped him into the river Styx as an infant in order to grant him immortality. She held him by the heel and this is the exact spot that Paris shot under the guidance of the god Apollo.

Odysseus was also able to abduct the prophetic son of King Priam, Helenus. He foretold that the Greeks will not win unless Achilles' son Pyrrhus joined the war, the bow and arrows of Hercules were used, the remains of the hero Pelops were brought to Troy, and the Palladium was stolen from the city. The Greeks were able to accomplish all of this.

Then, in order to enter Troy, Odysseus, with the inspiration of the goddess Athena, thought of building a large wooden horse. The inside of the horse would be hollow and could hide soldiers inside.

The artist Epeius created the horse—now popularly known as the Trojan Horse. Odysseus along with some men climbed inside. The Greek fleet sailed away to trick the Trojans into thinking that they have left. One Greek was left behind, a man named Sinon. The Trojans came out to behold the large horse as Sinon pretended to be furious with the Greeks for abandoning him. He gained the trust of the Trojans and assured them that the horse was good luck. Celebrating what they thought was finally their victory, the Trojans took the horse within the walls of the city. Later that night when the city was asleep after a long day of celebration, Sinon opened the horse and let his comrades out. The Greeks slaughtered many Trojans including King Priam. Menelaus was able to take back his wife Helen. He wanted to kill her, but upon seeing her face again, he was taken again by her beauty and let her live.

The Trojan War ended and the Greeks set off for home. The ensuing adventures are narrated in Homer's Odyssey. The journey back for most of the men was as long and difficult as the war itself.

Chapter 8: Pygmalion and Galatea

Pygmalion was known in ancient Greece as one of the best sculptors around. He was also known to have a dislike for women after witnessing how the immoral Propoetides, daughters of Propoetus, prostituted themselves. The Propoetides were punished by Venus for not acknowledging her as a goddess. They became the first ever prostitutes who sold their bodies without shame.

Pygmalion's views would be drastically changed after he created his best sculpture ever. This one he made from a large piece of perfect ivory. Pygmalion made a statue of a beautiful woman from the ivory and named it Galatea, meaning, "sleeping love". The sculptor quickly fell head over heels with his statue. He dressed it in beautiful clothes and adorned it with jewels.

The sculptor, who had no wife then, asked Aphrodite during the goddess' festival day for one that resembled his most prized creation—his "ivory girl". The goddess was intrigued and visited the home of Pygmalion. She found the statue to be beautiful and similar to her likeness so she gave the statue life. Upon his return, Pygmalion kissed the statue and was surprised to feel that it was warm. He then saw that his masterpiece slowly became a living, breathing beautiful woman. He was so delighted that he kneeled at Galatea's feet.

The two got married and expressed their gratitude by bringing gifts regularly to the temple of the goddess. They had a son who they named after the city -- Paphos. Another account of their story stated that the couple had a daughter named Metharme.

Chapter 9: Hyacinth

Hyacinth was a young prince of Sparta known for his handsome looks. He was also called Hyacinthus and Hyakinthos. The Spartan prince was well-loved by the gods, particularly Apollo and Zephyros.

Hyacinth was the son of Pierus, the king of Macedon, and Clio. Pierus was the son of Magnes (son of Zeus and Thyia) and Meliboea (for whom the town in Thessaly was named after). Clio or Kleio is one of the nine Muses borne to Zeus and Mnemosyne. Clio is the muse or goddess of history or lyre playing, depending on which account you are reading.

One account declares King Oebalus of Sparta as Hyacinth's father while another states that he was the son of the Spartan King Amyclas. Oebalus was the son of Cynortas and husband to Princess Gorgophone, daughter of Perseus. Amyclas of Sparta, meanwhile, was borne to King Lacedemon (Lakedaimon) and Queen Sparta from whom the famous city is believed to be named after. Hyacinth, if he is indeed the son of Amyclas, is the brother of King Cynortas and Argalus and sister of Daphne (borne to Queen Diomede). Hyacinth is known to have had a sister named Polyboea.

The handsome Hyacinth was believed to be Apollo's lover, which made Zephyr jealous. The West Wind, himself, revered the young man and this caused a feud between the two gods. The story of Hyacinth's death was tragic, to say the least. Hyacinth, who favored Apollo over Zephyr, was unfortunately killed in an accident. He and Apollo were throwing a discus when Hyacinth decided to impress the god. He ran after the discus Apollo threw hoping to catch it. However, the discus hit the young prince instantly killing him. Apollo tried to save Hyacinth by using his knowledge of herbal medicine but it was to no avail. According to other versions of the story, his death was not an accident. Zephyros or Zephyr, wind god that he was, became so jealous of Hyacinth and Apollo that he used his power to blow the discus off its course and hit the prince in the head.

Upon Hyacinth's death, Apollo was inconsolable. He prevented Hades, the god of the underworld, from taking Hyacinth. Hades relented and Apollo made a flower grown from the fallen man's blood. The larkspur flower (named after Hyacinth) was inscribed with the Greek words "Aiai" which is an exclamation of grief. This was according to Publius Ovidius Naso, a poet who could see things that other ordinary people couldn't see. Another version says Hyacinth and his sister Polyboea, who died a virgin, was taken to Elysium or heaven by the gods Aphrodite, Artemis, and Athena.

Hyacinth's tomb can be found in Amyclae, the city where a festival (Hyacinthia) was held by the people of Lacedaemonia in honor of the two lovers. His tomb sits beneath the image of Apollo.

The love story between Apollo and Hyacinth is perhaps the most well-known relationship between a male god and another male figure. However, the first ever depiction of two men having a relationship was between Hyacinth and Thamyris. Thamyris was the son of Philammon and Argiope, a nymph.

He was a well-known singer from Thrace who boasted that he was better than the Muses. He challenged the Muses to a musical contest in which he could enjoy them if he won and the Muses can do whatever they wish to him if they won. Thamyris lost and was punished by making him blind and unable to write poems and play music. It is believed that his punishment for boasting was carried over to the underworld after his death.

Chapter 10:
Procne and Philomena

Among the minor characters in Greek mythology, few can compare to the unfortunate event that happened to the two sisters, Procne and Philomena. While considered less important than other Greek characters, the story of the sisters is well known.

Procne and Philomena were the daughters of Pandion I, one of the kings of Athens. The legendary king comes from an important lineage having been born to Erichthonius and Praxithea. The sisters' great grandfather was Hephaestus, the Greek god of artisans, sculptors, metallurgy, fire, and blacksmiths, who was tasked with making the weapons used by the gods in Olympus. That makes the king and queen of the gods, Zeus and Hera, the sisters' great-great grandparents.

Procne and Philomena's grandfather was another legendary king of Athens who was born of the Earth. Erichthonius was raised by no less than the goddess Athena herself. Their grandmother Praxithea was a Naiad nymph. There are four other Greek mythology characters that went by the name Praxithea. One was the wife of Erechtheus II, the son and heir of King Pandion I. Another was daughter to Leos who sacrificed her and his two other daughters to save Athens. Thespius and Megamede had fifty daughters, one of which – Praxithea – gave birth to Nephus, son of Heracles. The last

Praxithea was Queen Metanira's maid who unwittingly prevented Demophon (King Celeus and Metanira's son) from becoming a god. Other versions of the story tell that Metabira herself was the woman who cried upon seeing Demeter holding Demophon by the fires during a ritual to turn the mortal boy into an immortal.

The Naiad Praxithea had a sister named Zeuxippe who eventually married Pandion. In other words, Pandion married his aunt Zeuxippe. They had four children. Aside from Procne and Philomela, they also had twin sons Erechteus and Butes.

Procne, the eldest of King Pandion's daughters, married King Tereus of Thrace. Tereus was the son of Ares, the Greek god of war. He was one of more or less 58 children borne to Ares. The identity of Tereus' mother was never revealed as were those of eight other children of Ares. Tereus and Procne had a son they named Itys, sometimes referred to as Itylos.

Procne moved to Thrace with Terues after they were married. Five years passed and Procne was deeply longing for her sister Philomena. She asked her husband to pay Philomena a visit and ask her to come with him to Thrace. Philomena is known for her beauty. She was so beautiful that many were captivated by her. Even Tereus was tempted by Philomena's beauty. On their way to Thrace, Tereus forced himself on Philomena. After the ghastly deed, Tereus feared that his wife would find out that he raped her sister. To prevent Philomena from telling anyone, Tereus tore her tongue out. He also hid Philomena so no one would ever find out. One account says Tereus dressed Philomena as a male servant to hide her. But that did not deter Philomena from seeking her sister to tell her the truth.

Philomena made a tapestry (or a robe according to some accounts) which revealed the ungodly events that took place.

She then asked an elderly woman to go to Thrace and give the tapestry to Procne. Once she saw the tapestry, Procne came to her sister's recue with the help of the old woman. Once together, the sisters plotted their revenge on Tereus.

Knowing how Tereus adored his son Itys, Procne figured out that the best revenge would be to kill him. But they didn't simply kill her son, they beheaded him. Itys' body was then cooked and served to the treacherous Tereus for supper. Tereus consumed his meal not knowing he was eating his own son. After the meal, Philomena showed herself to the king and threw his son's severed head on the very table he ate on.

Tereus, obviously enraged by what transpired, grabbed an axe and chased the sisters with the intentions of killing them. Tereus was able to catch up with the sisters at Daulia in Phocis. But before he could slay them, the sisters prayed to the gods for help. The gods (probably Apollo) answered their prayers and they were turned into birds. Procne became a swallow while Philomena transformed into a nightingale. Tereus didn't escape the gods as he was also turned into a bird – a hoophoe (a hawk in other versions of the story).

The story of the sisters and Tereus would be the subject of a number of plays. Sophocles, the famous author of *Antigone* and *Oedipus Rex*, wrote a play entitled Tereus. The tragic poet Philocles wrote a Pandionis tetralogy with a play about Tereus and the sisters being one of them. The canonic poet Ovid depicted the story in *Metamorphoses* while the great playwright Williams Shakespeare wrote *Titus Andronicus* which mentioned the Greek tragedy. Two characters in his play, Chiron and Demetrius, cut off the tongue (and hands) of Lavinia after raping her. Timberlake Wertenbaker also adapted the story as a play entitled *The Love of the Nightingale* while Richard Mills made the play into an opera.

Aristophanes, a poet from Athens, also parodied their story in *The Birds*. Fragments of his lost play were recovered and studied. David Fitzpatrick of Trinity College in Dublin, reconstructed Aristophanes' play using the recovered fragments. Fitzpatrick's interpretation depicts the wrongdoings of all main characters. According to him, a *deus ex machina*, believed to be Apollo, turned the trio into birds and proceeds to say that "any mortal who is infuriated by his wrongs and applies a medicine that is worse than the disease is a doctor who does not understand the trouble."

Chapter 11: Prometheus and Pandora

The brothers Prometheus and Epimetheus were Titans. The name "Prometheus" can be translated to "forethought" and he always was thinking of the future and making plans to make the world better and wiser. The younger "Epimetheus" is derived from "afterthought" for he was always thinking of what had already past and didn't bother himself with what was yet to come.

Prometheus loved mankind and went to live with them in order to help them. He found out that they were living in poor conditions, starving with nothing to eat, dying from the cold of the caves and ground they lived in, and being hunted by wild beasts at night as they slept. Prometheus, being wise, realized that what man needed the most was fire. So, he asked Zeus to grant men the gift of fire. Zeus disagreed for he reasoned that fire will make man stronger and wiser, and this could lead to them opposing the rule of the gods. It is for the best of the gods that they remained ignorant.

One day, as he was walking along a seashore, he found a reed. When he broke it, he found that the inside was filled with dry pith that would burn slow for a long time. He took this stalk to where the sun lies in the East and touched the reed to its flames. He carried the burning stalk back to men who were shivering in a cold cave and made a fire for them. He taught them how to make other fires and the things they could do with it. The men became very happy.

After that, he taught them even more useful things like how to build houses and how to tame cattle and sheep for use in farming. He taught them mining and metalwork so they could produce items for use every day and in the event of war. The world was coming into a bright Golden Age.

Zeus, on his mighty throne, happened to look down on the world below and saw fires burning, people living in wooden and stone houses, and farms bearing crops and fruits. What he saw made him furious. He asked for the culprit and found out that it was all because of Prometheus. He wanted to punish them, but first, he decided to make men miserable.

He ordered the blacksmith Hephaestus to mold a lump of clay into a woman. When the form was finished, he brought it to Zeus. The mighty god bid all the other gods to bestow upon the figure different gifts. Zeus gave it life. One gave her beauty, the other talent, and another gave her goodness, while the last one gave her curiosity. They named her Pandora, a name which can be loosely translated to "one who has all gifts." She was the first woman ever created, and she was beautiful and kind. Everyone could not help but love her. Zeus, then, ordered Hermes to give her to Epimetheus to be his wife. Prometheus was suspicious of the gift and warned his brother to take precaution. Epimetheus, recognizing how perfect a creature she is, did not heed his warning. He took her home and made her his wife.

Zeus sent Pandora away with a golden jar (thought to be a box in later versions), and told her that it contained many wonderful things. Athena, the wisest of them all, told Pandora to never open it.

Ever curious, Pandora wondered everyday what that jar might contain. She thought they could be jewels, which made her want to open it. Thinking that it would not hurt to peek just a little, she opened the lid slightly. But suddenly, out flew thousands of horrible-looking creatures that went out into the world. These were diseases, plagues and troubles that settled onto men as they peacefully slept in their homes. She shut the lid closed, but it was too late. Mankind could no longer become happy.

Devastated by what she had done, she wept until her husband found her. She took the lid off the jar to show him that it was empty. However, a tiny creature was left inside and was able to come out and fly into the world. The creature was Hope, and it made all the difference.

Next, Zeus came after Prometheus for his treachery. His crime was that he stole fire from the sun. He ordered that the young titan be carried to the highest peak of the Caucasus Mountains, and he told Hephaestus to chain him to the rocks so that he could not escape or move.

Prometheus spent the ages hanging there, unrepentant. The harsh winds and clawing of eagles did nothing to weaken his resolve. Sometimes, fair creatures would bring him messages from faraway lands or offer beautiful songs to him. Men could also look up and see him where he was, and they took pity on their friend who suffered the wrath of the mighty Zeus.

Conclusion

Thank you again for downloading this book!

I hope this book was able to help you learn more about Greek Mythology and its history!

Finally, if you enjoyed this book, please take the time to share your thoughts and post a review on Amazon. It'd be greatly appreciated!

Thank you and good luck!

www.ingramcontent.com/pod-product-compliance
Lightning Source LLC
LaVergne TN
LVHW021735060526
838200LV00052B/3280